★POLITICS★
THE STARTER KIT

HOW TO
SUCCEED
IN POLITICS AND
GOVERNMENT

JIM NOWLAN

authorHOUSE®

AuthorHouse™
1663 Liberty Drive
Bloomington, IN 47403
www.authorhouse.com
Phone: 833-262-8899

Published by AuthorHouse 06/20/2023

ISBN: 979-8-8230-1019-1 (sc)
ISBN: 979-8-8230-1020-7 (e)

Library of Congress Control Number: 2023911294

Print information available on the last page.

CONTENTS

Preface vii

Chapter 1:   Understanding Politics: The Struggle for
             Power and Influence................................. 1

Chapter 2:   How Do I Get into Politics?........................ 9

Chapter 3:   How Do I Run for Office? 15

Chapter 4:   The Successful Lawmaker 27

Chapter 5:   The Effective Legislative Staffer................. 35

Chapter 6:   Government Management: Practical
             Guidance for New Agency Directors 39

Chapter 7:   Everybody's a Lobbyist!........................... 45

Chapter 8:   Corruption: I Didn't Plan to Be Unethical......... 52

Chapter 9:   Is There a Future for You in Politics and Government?.... 57

For further reading..61

Acknowledgements.. 63

Jim Nowlan biographical sketch................................ 65

Endnotes.. 67

HOW TO SUCCEED IN POLITICS AND GOVERNMENT

This book is for persons new to politics and government, or who are interested in becoming involved. The goal is to provide "how to" guidance and lessons learned that can help you succeed in public life. This is a "starter kit." I draw in part on my own career over half a century in Illinois and D.C.—as an intern; legislative staffer; state legislator; statewide candidate; senior aide to three governors of Illinois; state agency director on three occasions; campaign manager for a U.S. senator (successful) and presidential candidate (interesting); lobbyist; newspaper columnist, and professor (see bio sketch at back).

I have been personally involved in politics and government with scores of effective politicians, from Richard M. Nixon during his "wilderness year" of 1966, to Illinois state senator Barack Obama at the beginning of the 21st Century. I do not know everything, of course, so I have talked with dozens of savvy politicians and government executives for lessons from their experiences.

This is the book I wish I had read when I was getting started in politics.

In the chapters that follow, I focus first on the dynamics of getting into politics and running for office. Then I discuss the challenges of trying to achieve one's objectives when in legislative and executive positions. This book is about "how to do" rather than "what to do."

I hold moderate Republican political values that I consider sound, yet this brief work is not about philosophy, other than the critical importance of responsible politics and government for a healthy democratic society. The world in 2023 is in the throes of rapid change, a world far removed from that of more than half a century ago, when I began in politics and government. The broad middle of the philosophical spectrum that I remember has fragmented, and the dominant forces in local, state and national politics are often at the polar ends of the Left and Right. Anger seems to be replacing compromise. Finding common ground is proving difficult.

Conservatives have generally resisted change, while liberals have seen the world as it as they wish it to be, often promoting change to achieve their objectives. There is much to be said for the pragmatism of the former, and the idealism of the latter. Both are needed. Yet the terms conservative and liberal are today not always appropriate when applied to American politics. For example, many conservatives find themselves allied in the Republican Party with populists, who challenge the elite (a category in which conservatives used to be comfortable).

I hope that those who are intrigued with the tumult of today's politics, maybe you, will see the problems confronting American democracy as a challenge, an avocation or even a vocation by which to make your positive mark in support of our society.

CHAPTER 1

UNDERSTANDING POLITICS: THE STRUGGLE FOR POWER AND INFLUENCE

"How does Stark County vote?" intoned the chair of the nominating convention. "Stark County casts five votes for the Honorable John T. Culbertson," I responded, my voice quavering. After all, I was a college freshman, and the hotel ballroom in Peoria was packed with delegates from 30 counties. Our job at this Republican convention was to nominate a supreme court justice onto the ballot. That's how it was done years ago in Illinois.

The county chair in my rural home county had heard I was active in student government, and he was friends with my Dad. So, he invited me to be one of five delegates to the meeting, even to cast our votes. The chair reserved a room at the hotel. The several judicial candidates each came by our room to make their pitch as to why they were best suited to sit on the state's highest court. It was heady stuff. I was participating in something big, I thought. I was hooked on politics from that day forward.

I wish I had this small book back then. I might have avoided some costly mistakes, and gotten a leg up on my contemporaries. If you decide you might have an interest in politics and government, access to the arena is easier than ever. Our major political parties are weaker than ever. County and neighborhood party chairs and candidates need volunteers more than ever.

Politics is the route into government, which exists to resolve conflict, and to seek order, harmony and prosperity in society. Important stuff. The 17th Century political thinker Thomas Hobbes admonished us: Without government, life would be solitary, poor, nasty, brutish and short.[1]

Politics is about the struggle for power and influence. I think of power as the capacity to force someone else to do something he might otherwise not have done. Influence is the ability to persuade another person to do something he was not planning otherwise to do.

As Franklin D. Roosevelt adviser and newspaper columnist Raymond Moley observed decades ago: "Politics is not something to avoid, abolish, or destroy. It is a condition like the atmosphere we breathe. It is something to live with, to influence if we wish and to control if we can. Either we must master its ways, or we shall be mastered by those who do."[2]

As with life, politics and "the struggle" represent a serious game in which each player tries to achieve his objectives, in collaboration with like-minded people, and in opposition or conflict with those whose objectives are different. Many people who get into politics enjoy this game, which is often lively, even fun. A lobbyist friend, who loved the game of getting his clients' bills passed, observes: "Politics is football without muscles."

When I was a professor, students asked: Which level of government is most important? I responded that while international and national politics might seem the most exciting of pursuits, each level has its own singular importance. Each is "most important," depending upon the situation.

When sewage is backing up in your basement because of a snafu with underground municipal plumbing, which is more important to the homeowner at the time: your city government, or relations with China? Indeed, most of the critical day-to-day activities of a family's life—public safety, education, college-going, transportation, healthcare, social services —are provided by the states and their local governments.

POLITICS, PHILOSOPHY, PSYCHOLOGY INTERTWINED

Why do politicians pursue politics? Basically, though it sounds clinical, it's because the human animal seeks power and influence for purposes of increasing his "fitness," that is, his attractiveness to others, especially to prospective mates. This quest is not all that different from the childhood game of "king of the hill," where players try to ascend to the top of the hill, pushing competitors aside, and even down the hill.

Philosophy is the study of wisdom, which can be seen as the search for an understanding of "What matters?"; "How should I live my life?" and also, apropos of politics: "How should I apply whatever power and influence I can gather?"

Throughout history, thinkers have examined these questions by observation and speculation. The most famously practical of these old-world treatises is *The Prince* by Niccolò Machiavelli. He offers the Medici, the dominant political family of Renaissance Florence, a handbook on how to expand its power, survive and flourish against those who would try to dislodge the family from the pinnacle of the hill. Niccolò offers brutally practical, some would say cynical, guidance, which is why we speak of Machiavellian politics.[3]

> Lawmakers like to do things *for* voters, and not *to* voters.

Politics is complex. The "chessboard" of politics is without defined boundaries. There are thousands of elected officials, candidates, volunteers and donors, each with unique moves, in a multitude of overlapping political arenas. Yet politics is somewhat predictable, because people are driven by fairly well understood needs and passions. For example, an enduring behavioral trait among elected officials: Lawmakers like to do things *for* voters, and not *to* voters–as in spending *for* programs and *against* taxes to pay for them. That is why government continues to expand, and many governments run deficits. Figuring out these likely moves of others, that is, predicting their behavior, through evaluation of their needs and end games, is a key to success in politics.

Politicians tend to like other people, enjoy interacting with them. The late Illinois governor Jim Thompson (1977-1991) was in his element drinking peppermint schnapps from a toilet plunger with fraternity boys at a college football game. Most love, some even need, the feedback that socializing on the campaign trail brings. Though not always. Former president Richard M. Nixon and U.S. Sen. Adlai Stevenson of Illinois had to clench their teeth to wade through a campaign crowd.

The fundamental drives are the same anywhere: the Chicago City Council, the state legislature, or Congress, the Parliament of the United Kingdom, the one-house legislature of Costa Rica. However, varied cultural norms developed over many generations cause each arena to operate differently from the next. For example, some cultures tolerate corruption; others, not at all. My state of Illinois is reputed to have a tradition of political corruption. Getting politicians to fix a DUI violation used to be almost common practice in many Chicago and Downstate rural neighborhoods. Nearby Iowans and Minnesotans would generally be aghast at the idea, and more importantly, wouldn't be offered the opportunity to have the charge fixed. Different learned behaviors, that is, cultures.

If it is okay to fix a DUI, it is but a small step to using political influence to get the inside track on a juicy state contract for your business. There is less of this now than when I was a young lawmaker half a century ago, which also makes the point that cultures can and do change over time. A knowledge and sensitivity to the political culture in which you operate is important to navigating the minefields of politics. It doesn't mean you have to adopt corrupt values, of course, but to be aware of them. Avoid doing something simply "because that's the way things are done."

Most people in politics have ambition to succeed at their craft, ideally to move up the ladder. Politics is indeed a craft like carpentry or plumbing, learned through study and practice. And the political ladder is not that tall. There are only three basic steps on the ladder from the elected school board to the U. S. presidency: from local school board, city council or community activist to the state legislature (step 1); to Congress (step 2), and to the Presidency (step 3). Illustration: former President Barack Obama. Mr. Obama was active in Chicago community organizing, ran successfully for the state legislature, failed in his first run for Congress, but was elected to the U.S. Senate, and of course, ascended to the Presidency.

Politics is about behavior: voting—in elections, and in legislative chambers; making campaign contributions; volunteering in behalf of candidates; protesting of the streets. To be good at politics, you need to understand as best you can what is going on in the minds of others.

That is, the thinking that drives behavior. It isn't always what people say, but what they are thinking that will determine their behavior. The late, legendary Chicago mayor Richard J. Daley was infamous for his garbled syntax. Following some news stories he didn't like, he reportedly criticized the press: Don't print what I say. Print what I mean!

So, to understand how others see the world, you have to know at least a bit about how the brain works. Here is a brief, yet important illustration about racism and, related, the powerful "us versus them" drivers in our brain:

As I write this in 2023, I read about high-profile incidents of violence against Blacks, Jews, Asian-Americans. This prompts the question: Are Americans racist? My response: Of course, we are, tragically, in this sense: The brain of the human animal became, over six million years of experience at survival games, hardwired to predispose people to see one another as of two kinds—"us versus them." This is obviously not to excuse racism, but to try to understand it, and to appreciate the importance of understanding basic human behaviors.

According to Stanford neuroscientist Robert Sapolski, a skin color different from our own immediately lights up the brain when you, I, and most people scan the world around us.[4] Our brain is divided, very roughly, into three compartments. At the base of the brain is the stem, which guides our basic bodily functions. In the middle of our cranium are several interconnected brain parts that govern our emotions, and our "flight or fight" responses to threats. Forward in the brain is our frontal cortex, a late comer, you might say, to our brain. The prefrontal cortex is the "thinking" part of our being.

These three parts of the brain are in continuous interaction, firing neuronal signals back and forth and all around, constantly. Based on millions of years of experience at survival, the central part of the brain is powerful, really powerful. The more recent frontal cortex "advises" the central part on how to behave. Sometimes, but not always, the frontal cortex is successful at overriding the central part. For example, there might be an override when the brain's initial "gut reaction" is to lash out at a perceived, but not real, threat. "Calm down. Take a deep breath," our prefrontal cortex shouts to the central brain. The more time the front part of the brain has to intervene before actions are taken, the better.

Now that you understand the brain :-), let's zero in on racism, that is, belief in the odiousness or inferiority of the "thems." The brain is predisposed to think this way all the time, e.g., whites are superior to blacks; Israelis are superior to Palestinians; farmers are superior to city folk; black athletes are superior to white jocks; the Cubs are superior to the Cardinals (well, this last is a stretch, but the brain believes it).

The more distant a "them" group, or the less we know about it, the easier it is to believe that group is obnoxious or inferior. On the other hand, if a white household has lived comfortably for years next to a black family, our us-versus-them feeling often becomes sharply diminished. It's called "getting to know you."

There is some good news. We continue to evolve, generally in the right direction. I am amazed, for example, at how quickly attitudes have changed, in just recent decades, about sexual orientations. When I was a kid in the 1950s, my father was among our small town's leading citizens. These leading men literally ran a new school teacher out of town, when it was rumored that he was "queer." My sister, then a student, said he was a great teacher, whom all the kids liked.

Fortunately, we have generally moved far beyond that kind of incredibly cruel them-bashing. But for the coming decades, "gut" racism among many people is not likely to recede completely, of its own accord. The challenge for society is to rewire our brains to see the world as made up of one kind of people–humans. This will take time. We must develop strategies to convince the brains of racists that they should focus on the individual, rather than on the group.

For example, the Illinois Farm Bureau does this quite effectively with its longstanding "Adopt a Legislator (meaning urban lawmaker) Program." Weekend visits for an urban legislator and his or her family are hosted on the farm, and there are often reciprocal visits in the city. Barriers come down, at least somewhat, as a result. "Getting to know you" can work.

Having an appreciation for "the political system" is also important. The late political scientist Robert Easton sketched the political system as a rather simple input-output world. (See political system graphic nearby.)[5]

The Political System
Thanks to David Easton

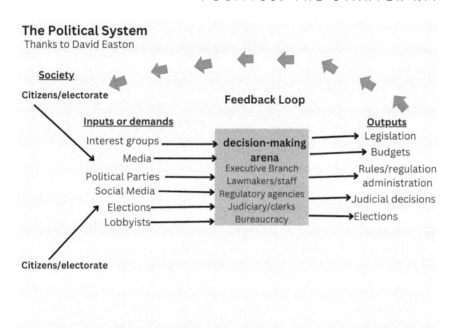

If those in the decision-making box are unable to satisfy enough demands, the political system risks collapse, overthrow. As a graduate student, I found Easton's rather simple schema persuasive, and still do, as a way of standing back to understand what is going on.

* * *

Each player in the game of politics has a bundle of resources, small or large, which he or she is always trying to expand.

The ballpark of politics is defined by constitutions, laws, rules, and the norms and values of the players. Each player brings his own bundle of resources to the game. A president or governor has a huge bundle of powers and influence based upon his office, constitutional authority, skills that brought him into office, public visibility, and more. At the other end of the spectrum might be the greenest, newly elected member of a legislative body, whether city council, state legislature or U.S. Congress. Yet even this freshman has a small bundle: He has, for example, his vote, which chief executives, legislative leaders and fellow lawmakers will all need at some point. The freshman legislator may also bring expert knowledge from business, construction, higher education or whatever to the political arena. Information is important, and craved, in politics.

The challenge for the new lawmaker is to build his bundle of power and influence over time. He can do this in various ways. Politics is largely a game of debits and credits, and of reciprocity. The new lawmaker husbands his credit-generating actions by his votes in committee and on the legislative floor. He or she builds credits by doing favors, tiny and large, for fellow legislators, and addressing the needs and vulnerabilities of others in the game.

> Politics is largely a game of debits and credits, and of reciprocity.

To illustrate: With consummate skill at applying limited resources combined with exquisite understanding of the needs of his fellow senators, Lyndon Johnson became majority leader of the U.S. Senate–after just two years as a senator, an unprecedented achievement in a slow-moving, tradition-encrusted body.[6]

So, if this introduction sparks any interest, the following chapter offers guidance as to how to get into politics.

CHAPTER 2

HOW DO I GET INTO POLITICS?

As a professor of politics, I was asked by more than one student, "How do I get into politics?" Your first task is to assess whether you are cut out for public life. It isn't for everyone. For most, but not all, jobs in politics and public service you have to like people, get a kick out of socializing with them, and enjoy learning from them. There are exceptions. As noted in Chapter 1, our late president Richard M. Nixon loved the game of strategizing about politics, yet, based on my personal knowledge, I don't think he really enjoyed people that much. Yet, because of his obsession with proving himself in a profession for which he wasn't perfectly suited, he succeeded impressively, for a while, until his impeachment and resignation.

If you think you would enjoy politics, but you aren't the "front-man type," there are important roles in addition to being the candidate and elected official. These include campaign management, as well as staff roles with a state legislator, member of Congress, governor, Congress, the White House. Politics is a team game.

If you are at present a student, you can gain experience via student government and organizations such as College Democrats or Republicans. Entry is easy, and you can, in effect, practice politics and government. As a College Republican, I went to regional and national conventions, where what we did mirrored what real politicians do. The experience also gave me an opportunity to observe what political junkies are like, that is, the young people who have already set their caps on careers in politics and government. You may find yourself a "junkie," obsessed with politics, or not. Junkies are not, by the way, necessarily likely to go further in politics than non-junkies. To me, it's more about personality, street smarts, and drive.

I know many who have interest in politics, yet decide first to pursue careers in the professions of law, medicine, business, and entrepreneurship. In the backs of their minds, they have harbored the idea that someday, when they have achieved a career to fall back upon, plus maybe financial security, they will pursue politics and public service.

There are many opportunities to "get into politics." You can volunteer with a political party organization, or for a candidate. If you really have gumption, you can become a candidate yourself. That's what my student Frank Calabrese did.

Frank became a candidate for the Illinois House, while a college student at the University of Illinois in Urbana-Champaign. Frank didn't expect to win, and he didn't. But he learned a lot about who the players were and how the game was played. He is now a big-time political consultant in Chicago. Another example: My friend Charles Owens, a middle-age pharmacist, now retired, had never been involved in politics. Yet, he ran for lieutenant governor in an Illinois Republican primary. He didn't win, either. But because he was on the ballot, he was included on the dais at all the endless candidate rallies he could reach, throughout the state. And he was allowed his three-minute speech, like all the other candidates. His issues, as a Catholic social activist, were homelessness and abortion. "I had a ball," Charles recounts. "All it cost me was travel money, and I espoused my issues to thousands more than I could ever do otherwise. And I got to know my state."

I don't recommend running for serious office right out of the gate. Better to volunteer with a local party organization or a candidate of the party of your choice. Political parties are formal organizations outside of government. Their job is to recruit candidates who support party values, then support their candidacies to elect them into government, where they can implement the party's values and positions.

The basic unit of the party organization is the precinct, a voting district with around 500 to 1,500 registered voters. Generally, a precinct is represented by a precinct committeeperson. In some states, this person is elected within the party at the biennial primary election. If they are elected where you vote, you can run for the precinct post from the get go, and generally be appreciated by the county or city ward party leader for doing so. In others, this precinct representative is appointed by, say, a county party leader, and there are often vacancies to be filled. The sum of the precinct committeepersons in a county comprises the county party committee. This committee elects the county chair and often participates in naming replacements for seats in the legislature that have been vacated. County parties that meet regularly offer you opportunities to observe what is going on in local politics.

The task of the precinct committeeperson is to take party values to the voters in the precinct, and encourage voters to go to the polls to vote for the party's candidates. Some county parties endorse candidates for office when there are primary nomination contests. This is often done on the basis of a vote of the precinct committeepersons. The vote is often weighted to the party's vote for governor in each respective precinct, in a recent election. So, a precinct committeeperson who turns out a large party vote in his or her precinct has a bigger voice than one who doesn't. If you are able to increase the party vote in your precinct, you have more influence with your county chair, as you indirectly increase his influence on the county and state level.

Above the precinct is the pyramid of the county, state, and national party organizations. Persons really serious about politics often move up the ladder. It is possible to volunteer with both the party organization as well as the campaign organizations created by a candidate or an elected official. Indeed, candidate organizations like it when their people are also involved with the county party organization.

When I was a young politician 60 years ago, the county-level party committees were expected–and *they* expected–to run the local campaigns of candidates for city, county and state office. The county chair was an important player in politics. He (they were almost all male back then) raised money, nominated people in his organization to hold paid patronage jobs in various governments, and assisted citizens with their needs and problems with government.

Today, a paid job awarded for party work is rare, though not extinct. As a result, there is less vested interest in serving as a precinct committeeman, at least doing so in hopes of a patronage job on the highway crew or with the state department of agriculture. Most such party jobs are prohibited by a 1990 U.S. Supreme Court decision, *Rutan v. the Republican Party of Illinois*, 1990. Patronage workers also contributed some of their pay to the party organization, which helped keep the county party important.[7]

For these and related reasons, the party organization is in most places less important today than it was in my day. That is why there are so many precinct posts vacant, and so many opportunities for you to participate. As a result of party weakness in many areas, candidates and officials often have to develop their own personal organizations of volunteers, skilled campaigners and donors.

Party organizations tend to be more important in state capitals, where politics and government may be the biggest "industry." They are also active in some urban communities where politics has traditionally been almost a blood sport. County party posts are often much sought after in these worlds, yet there are still opportunities for you as a volunteer, maybe even a precinct committeeman(woman) or "precinct captain." Volunteers can be critical: door knocking (also called canvassing), putting out mailings, helping at events, walking in parades; driving for a candidate (which is a great way to develop relationships with numero uno); graphic arts and IT skills; research; even membership as part of a large, extended family clan, and the capacity to recruit other volunteers. When offering to volunteer, make it clear what skills you bring to the party or candidate.

If you offer to volunteer, be certain you can pitch in when you are needed. If you offer to volunteer, and fail to do so when called upon, you are basically useless in politics. When I was running major campaigns for statewide office, my team and I once observed that only about one in ten persons who volunteer actually end up being of help when needed. So, if you bust your tail helping, you will be–or should be–much appreciated. And this will increase your chances of moving up the rungs at some point to a paid position, should that be your objective.

Volunteering is a good learning experience. You come to learn that people overall have very little knowledge of offices to be filled and of the issues. You also learn that most people who answer the doorbell (many do not) are pleased that you would take time to give them information about your candidate. And you build people skills.

When I was a young man, I would have said: Depending upon your value preference, go to your local political party organization, say, the Johnson County Democratic Central Committee and offer to volunteer. As noted, many party organizations have declined in activity and influence over the years. As a result, candidates and elected officials now often have to build their own organizations, where you can volunteer instead, or also.

THIRD PARTY AND INDEPENDENT POLITICS OFFER OPPORTUNITIES

In 2023, as I write, many citizens are unhappy with both of our major political parties. There is the option of supporting or becoming an Independent or third-party candidate. Even though such candidacies tend to fail, these activities have a role in politics. For example, the Republican Party was in the 1850s a new, third party. Over the course of four, two-year election cycles it became a major party, supplanting the Whig Party. In the 19th and 20th centuries, the Socialist Party of America espoused social security and universal health care policies long before they were adopted by the Democratic Party.

Outside political parties, a person can learn about politics by becoming active in the political action committees of interest groups. For example, urban community organizations, county Farm Bureaus, and union locals often have such committees. Environmental, climate change and social issues groups also work hard to influence politics and policy, and often welcome volunteers on public issues committees. Participating will increase your knowledge of issues of interest, and offer interaction with legislators in advocating for group interests. Labor unions, corporations, and even your employer might appreciate your offer to help with pertinent issues.

Internships with governments offer another excellent way to get into public life. Local, state and national governments offer an array of internships, a few of which are well paid, and for as long as a year. Internships for college graduates are tools governments use for recruiting into full time, career positions. In addition, they offer experience that is critical for professional work in lobbying and governmental relations.

If you are interested in working with the federal government, you cannot generally land a job without going to D.C. and knocking on the doors of congressional offices and agencies. They want to see you, hear you. For example, when I was directing a graduate program in public management, I had a fine student, who was also finishing a law degree. She came in to see me. She was not getting any responses to her mailed inquiries. This was the George H. W. Bush Administration (1989-93), and a time when gender and race were becoming important, especially to an administration that had less than its share of either. Here she was, a highly presentable African-American who spoke close-to-fluent French, after a year studying in Switzerland.

"You have to go to D.C. and knock on doors," I declared. She did. Her first stop was OMB (the White House Office of Management and Budget). Upon her return, I asked how her door-knocking went. "It didn't last long," she said. "OMB almost literally wouldn't let me out of its office until I committed to work for them." My student/friend has had a fine career in D.C., now at the U. S. Department of Justice in a rewarding role. The point: For politically oriented jobs in D.C., you have to go to them. They won't come to you!

Now that you have some ideas about how to get into politics and government, how do you run for office?

CHAPTER 3

HOW DO I RUN FOR OFFICE?

Before making a decision to run for office, some questions are in order. Why are you running? To further a cause, an issue? A longtime national political operative said people run for one or more of the "Three P" reasons: power, prestige, pecuniary (money). Maybe you find the challenge of the rough and tumble of politics intriguing, exciting. You might have a career in mind, either in politics, or as a stepping stone into lobbying. But, should you run? Political campaigns have often become nasty. Are you willing to have your name, even your family, besmirched unfairly? And, do you have "the right stuff"?

You must be willing to ask people for their help, and money. I found this excruciatingly hard to do, as a 24-year-old candidate for the Illinois Legislature. But, somehow, I did it. To ask people successfully for their financial support, you must first convince yourself that you will be doing them a service. You will be advocating, after all, for the betterment of their community, for a cause, for issues that are of importance to the fundraising prospect. You're selling yourself and what you can do for the world around you.

Can you afford to run? I have suggested to my students that they not consider running for a full-time elected job until they have first established financial independence, or an alternate career path, should the fickle game of politics send you out of office on your ear. Politics is an uncertain business. Tenure in office can be cut short unexpectedly by decennial redistricting, or by a fickle electorate.

On the other hand, some young people are restless to get in the game, and run for office, as I did, at 24. They reason that time is a wasting asset, and that they can learn soon enough if politics is for them and still have time to develop another career. The following brief sketch of running for office might be of help in deciding whether, and when.

THE RUN FOR OFFICE

You could become a candidate for local, state or national office. How much are you willing to bite off, initially? (For a more comprehensive account of how to run for and win election than can be offered here, see "Winning Elections" by Dick Simpson and coauthors, cited in the endnotes.[8]) What is your political "style"? Your style will be dictated largely by your personality, and your stomach for risk. As you consider running for office, you will often be counseled by party leaders to "wait your turn." I found that one's turn never seems to arrive, as others jump in ahead of you. I have also noticed other aspirants who kept waiting. . . and waiting. . . .until the time and opportunity were perfect—no strong opponents in the primary election and a clear path to victory in the fall general election. The perfect time rarely comes along. At some point, if you are really serious about running for office, you have to: 1) assess the situation; 2) determine whether there is a decent chance of success; 3) sketch a campaign plan that shows a route to success, and, 4) become a candidate.

I lay out here a run for office in the following hypothetical situation, which would have elements typical of many campaigns: A young man or woman, you were appointed two years ago to your county board of supervisors, to fill a vacancy. You have really enjoyed the issues, the people, the challenges, the game. As the next biennial round of elections approaches, you see there is an open seat for the state House of Representatives. You believe you would make a good, effective lawmaker. You decide to investigate the idea.

> ☆   ☆   ☆
>
> There are five fundamental resources in a political campaign: People, credibility, money, skill and time.

There are many questions you must answer: Might I have a chance of winning, first, the primary nomination of your party, and then the general election? Who would the likely opponents be? Where would I raise my campaign budget?

Abraham Lincoln said there were three tasks to a successful campaign: 1) Canvas your district, that is, get to know the district, its makeup, and its people. 2) Identify your voters, and 3) Get them to the polls. That's still pretty much the game.

There are five fundamental resources in a political campaign: People, credibility, money, skill and time. Each prospective candidate brings to the table at least some of one or more of these resources. For example: time, a wasting resource. Once a month is gone, it's gone, lost. So, candidates who start early and use their time efficiently have an advantage over those who don't, at least with regard to that resource.

The people in a campaign are you, your family and relatives, your friends, and others you rally to your candidacy. As noted earlier, political party organizations once ran the campaigns on behalf of their endorsed candidate. Because party organizations are much weaker today than several decades ago, candidates now often feel a need to build their own mini-organizations.

As for credibility, are you well known and respected in your community? Do you have respected friends and colleagues who will endorse your candidacy, especially elected or former officials? Your skills, as well as those of your friends and supporters, are obviously central to a campaign. Skills include: communicating and speaking, asking people for help and for money, and marketing your candidacy. For example, you or one of your volunteers may have experience with successful digital campaigning in your business or occupation; this skill has become required in campaigns. Digital communication and advertising are inexpensive and can be targeted to reach, almost laser-like, your target audience.

☆　　☆　　☆

"Money is the mother's milk of politics,"—former California Assembly speaker Jesse Unruh.

Money has been important in politics at least since English lords (and later George Washington in our American colonies), spent money "treating" their constituents to food and drink in their campaigns for Parliament. "Money is the mother's milk of politics," declared California

Assembly speaker Jesse Unruh decades ago. As a political consultant friend observed: 90 percent of the candidates who have more money than their opponents win. This means, obviously, that money is critical.[9] On the other hand, it is not always controlling, in at least one in ten campaigns. A candidate with less money than his opponent can sometimes win, especially if you have more of the other resources.

Half a century ago, I spent $4,000 in my first, unsuccessful campaign for the legislature. That is about $50,000 in 2023 dollars, which is but peanuts today in some big-state campaigns for the legislature. There was, for example, a state senate race in Illinois in 2022 that cost a total of $6 million. Yet, not all legislative races across the country are any more expensive today than mine was.

As noted earlier, I was awful at asking donors for contributions, and felt as if I were importuning prospective donors. Slowly, I gained confidence in myself. I had to. I needed the campaign funds. If you don't believe in yourself, you probably shouldn't be in politics. Salesmen are naturals at making pitches to donors, because they come to believe in their products. You need to look a prospective donor in the eye, and tell him an investment in your campaign will result in better government for him, and for society.

Today, you can research campaign donors and their donations at your state's board of elections website. This will tell you about whom your prospect contributes to, and how much. If he typically donates $250 to a candidate seeking the same kind of office as you are, then tell him you need his help, and ask for $500. He can always offer a smaller amount.

In my first campaign, I raised money as follows: A $5 per person chicken-and-beer fundraiser in an apartment near the campus where I was a graduate student. Lots of fun. And it energized fellow graduate students who felt good about coming up with $5 for the cause, when our teaching assistant stipends were but $200 a month.

Second, an uncle of mine hosted a cocktail reception at a private club in Chicago. Free-will donations from uncle's friends as well as from former undergraduate college classmates of mine, by then living in Chicago, probably averaged $10 (about $100 today). GOP friends in my rural home county also contributed. I also borrowed money as well, which is a bad idea for a young person, especially one without a career to fall back on.

A CAMPAIGN PLAN IS A MUST

You *must* have a written campaign plan. It doesn't have to be fancy. It does have to set forth a strategy by which you can win. It should be followed until it has to be changed. There are exogenous events during the campaign that you can't control, e.g., your opponent announces he has raised much more money than you expected, or a death in the immediate family of your opponent generates sympathy for him.

The plan tries to answer questions like this:

* How many votes do you need to win, and where in the district can you get them?
* What message(s), if any, will be important in generating votes?
* How will you build your team of politically savvy friends who know the district, plus inexperienced yet enthusiastic volunteers?
* How much time will you have to devote to campaigning?
* How much money will you need? One way to estimate this is to estimate how many times you and your message need to be seen by likely voters in your election? You can determine the cost by evaluating the cost of different marketing tools.
* Where can you raise the money? Obvious possibilities: yourself, extended family, friends, prominent people and businesses or labor unions, crowd-funding, fun fundraisers. Will the state legislative leader of your party back you, and how much money might your leader contribute (and how much support for him will you have to commit in return for that support)?
* How will you apply the campaign budget, that is, what is your marketing plan? Your campaign is in "the eyeball business." How do you reach the eyeballs of likely voters, and what are the respective costs per eyeball of the many marketing tools available? The traditional tools of major station TV, cable TV, radio and yard signs are being complemented, even replaced, by less expensive digital tools such as text messaging and programmatic digital ads, each of which can target your likely voters for pennies per eyeball. Today, in most states, you can identify the addresses of all the voters, by household, who cast ballots for the office you

seek in recent primary and general elections. Why waste money advertising to people who won't be voting in your race?

TARGETING IS THE NAME OF THE GAME

I chaired a five-county, local government election campaign in 2023. There were 250,000 people in the district, yet history told my committee and me that only about 1 in 30 adults would be voting in our extremely low-turnout off-year, down-ballot election. We had a budget of $15,000. We decided yard signs would be wasting our money to reach the vast majority who wouldn't be voting. Instead, we went with a 6x9" color mailer to every household that had voted previously in this off-year election. We complemented this with both text messages and multiple programmatic digital ads that targeted high propensity voters. Such voters have a high likelihood to vote in all elections, including ours. We believe we reached the eyeballs of most of the people who voted—more than a dozen times each. All for $15,000. Thirteen thousand votes were cast, and our two candidates won, one by just 40 votes.

THE CAMPAIGN

People think there are two stages in a campaign: the primary nomination and the general election. There is a third, sometimes even more critical stage, called the invisible pre-primary Months prior to circulating petitions to get on the ballot, prospective candidates jockey and preen, in efforts to scare all other candidates, maybe including you, out of running. If successful, this obviously creates a "free ride" to nomination, even election. Candidates with wealth, or with built-in major support, from a political leader or labor union, for example, have a greater chance of scaring others out than do those who lack big money. Yet sometimes a candidate can be successful in "winning" the pre-primary, even without big money. The candidate does this by displaying a big, enthusiastic base of volunteers and supporters, e.g. active membership in a large church congregation who will support you.

In a small, mostly or all-volunteer campaign, the candidate and manager may want to ask friends to serve, respectively, as chairs, respectively, of: fundraising; social media creator/manager; "field work" director (who generates and directs volunteers); Facebook campaign; yard sign organizer, whatever. This gives you a built-in team with which to meet regularly to assess how well the plan is being implemented and whether any tweaks are justified or needed.

Campaigning can be fun or excruciating, generally both. It's up to the candidate to set the tone. I strongly suggest the candidate make the campaign a joint effort, that is, involve as many people as possible, and make them feel they are a real part of your effort. Ask volunteers helpful questions they may be able to answer, such as: What is the mood of the electorate, what are the issues they are hearing about in the neighborhood pub, church or club?

SOME PRECINCT LEADERS CAN BE POWERFUL

The legendary skills of Chicago's politicians might give a false impression that strong political organizations have been the sole preserve of the urban Democrats. Not so. Getting out the vote is a result of cultural attitudes toward leadership and patrons, and here and there rural Illinois Republicans learned the tricks as well:

In my first try for office in 1966 I sought a Republican nomination for the Illinois House of Representatives from a rural district. Heeding the abundant advice given by old-timers, I paid a call on Louis Falletti, owner of a popular tavern and precinct committeeman for the small community of Italian Americans in and around the village of Dalzell in Bureau County, whose forebears had come to mine coal.

A courtly gentleman, Lou Falletti, received me graciously. But he told me bluntly he already had a candidate—and it wasn't me. Furthermore, I would not get a single vote in his precinct, Falletti said confidently. I left the Falletti home, adjacent to the tavern, vowing to prove him wrong. I spent more time and money in the precinct than planned. I walked door-to-door to introduce myself, even hanging around the popular Italian bakery, across the street from Faletti's chicken-and-spaghetti tavern, to say plead my case to residents.

I proved Lou Falletti wrong, you might say. Of 562 votes cast among six candidates, I received 10 votes. Falletti's candidate garnered 539.

Two years later I ran again. Falletti's candidates were not running this time, so he backed me in a four-way hotly contested race. I captured nearly all the votes in Dalzell this second time, and was elected to the House. Whenever Lou wanted help finding a job or doing a favor for one of his constituents, I busted my tail trying to get what Lou wanted![10]

There are traditional campaign activities you must master, such as:

How to develop positive relationships with people active in your political party. Visiting with county chairs and other political leaders, and communicating with precinct committeemen, is important. Precinct leader influence in his or her precinct ranges from significant to almost nonexistent. Yet, they and their families, and their extended families, will be voting, and their word of mouth can be valuable. They will also value being called upon, even if they aren't in a position to help you.

The three-minute stump speech (in the 19th Century, candidates would sometimes stand, we are told, on a tree stump to speak to—and be seen by—village voters). You will likely be invited to candidate rallies in your campaign, by the local party, neighborhood organizations, League of Women Voters, Farm Bureau, Chamber of Commerce. If you are allotted five minutes, use just three. These candidate forums can often be excruciatingly long, tedious for audiences. Audiences applaud brevity.

Make good use of your brief time at the dais. Tell the audience who you are; why you are running; who, if anyone, is backing you, and what you hope to accomplish. Simple as that. Audiences like a little self-effacing humor. (I would get a chuckle when I recounted that the big newspaper in my district in my first run referred to me as "Jim Toulon of Nowlan," when the reverse was actually the case.) But be aware that platform humor can be tricky. Humor can backfire badly. For example, if your good-natured comments about a local worthy might not be understood by others in the room, listeners might be offended.

"Work the room." At campaign events such as Lincoln Day or Jefferson-Jackson Day dinners, you must work the room, that is, go from table to table to introduce yourself. This was hard for me, initially. I lacked the personal confidence necessary; I felt I was bothering people at the tables. In fact, diners expect you to introduce yourself in person, and they appreciate shaking your hand. "Hi, I am Mary Smith, candidate for state rep. I'm from (your town). This is my first race, and I want to earn your vote." Sometimes this has to be done during the social hour that precedes the sit-down dinner. Same drill.

Knock on doors. There is software available today that tells you the voting records of people in each household, that is, whether they have voted recently, and what party ballot they requested in the primary nomination elections. This makes going door-to-door much more efficient than decades ago. Have a printed campaign card with you that has a hook on it, for hanging on doorknobs of the many households where no one answers the door.

When someone answers, be pleasant, thank them for coming to the door. Then get to the point: Who you are, what you are running for, and why you are running. Hand them your campaign card. Ask them for their vote, and whether they have any questions for you. If you have one specific issue you want to emphasize, tell them about it, briefly. If the householder is chatty, ask what issues he/she thinks are important for you to hear about. If the conversation is extended, ask the person if he or she might fill out a 3x5" volunteer card, with contact information. This way, you can communicate again.

Most of my experience has been in small city and rural as well as statewide and nationwide campaigns. For a comprehensive, detailed discussion of how to canvass in urban high-rise and suburban gated-community settings, which can often be difficult to maneuver, see the "Winning Elections" book, cited earlier in this chapter and as well as in the endnotes.

Never argue. Whether the exchange is minimal or more, thank the person for his time, and move on.

CAMPAIGN FUN FOR YOU AND YOUR FRIENDS

I enjoyed making a party out of doorbell work. I would gather friends on a Saturday afternoon. We would pair up, one for each side of the street. Friends can be quite effective campaigners, as it suggests you, the candidate, must have something going for you if friends are willing to take time to campaign for you. After a couple of hours in targeted neighborhoods, we would adjourn to a good pub, where I would host my friends for chicken and beer. We would have fun comparing notes about our experiences, and your friends would feel good about themselves, and become more invested in your campaign as a result of their efforts.

Call upon prominent people in your district. These are people who influence others, and who just might later contribute to your campaign. These people might be the president of the local bank, the head of the Rotary, leaders of urban community and neighborhood organizations, the Farm Bureau board, the school superintendent, commander of the American Legion. Request the opportunity to make a courtesy call on them. Even if they say they are too busy, your initiative will still go down well with them. The fact you consider them important enough to call upon suggests their importance.

Seek endorsements. Credibility is one of your most important resources. And since most voters are not likely to know you, as a newcomer to the game, the credibility of people who might publicly endorse you will be of great value. At the local level, this could be any well-known and respected persons and elected officials. Or, maybe a list of friends and neighbors. Even if not well known, the fact they are willing to sign a public letter or advertisement shows that your friends and neighbors respect you.

Say Thank You. Most people who participate are volunteers. They feel good about getting involved. Yet, they absolutely glow when the candidate looks them in the eye and tells them how much she values their work, how she couldn't succeed in politics without them. Politics is a team sport. If you don't think so, you probably won't go very far in the game.

CAMPAIGN MANAGEMENT CAN
BE EXHILARATING

I close this chapter with brief comments about managing campaigns for others. It's the same ballgame, but played in a bigger stadium. Somewhere along your path into public life, you may be asked to manage a political campaign, say, by a close friend who is a candidate. This might be as a volunteer, or a paid role. Without prior experience, for example, I was asked to manage the campaign of a U.S. senator who sought reelection in what proved to be a hotly contested race (I did have experience at running for office myself).

Campaign management can be exhilarating, even fun. You are, in effect, the conductor of a small orchestra. The campaign plan is your score, and the candidate is your soloist. The candidate has to do all the grunt work with the public, while the campaign manager is in the back office, implementing the plan.

For a statewide campaign, the manager basically creates a small business that operates for about a year, from pre-primary through the primary and general election. The manager may be both the chief operating officer as well as the brains of the campaign. Or, he may take the operating role while a professional political consultant(s) serve as the strategist and creative director.

Many of the key functions in a campaign are rented for the campaign year. Vendors can be found at the magazine *Campaigns & Elections*, or from local or district party leaders. C&E magazine has been the go-to place for insider dope about running campaigns since 1980. The magazine writes about all political services, including campaign consultant(s); survey research; fundraising; media relations; social media marketing.

A few words about campaign consultants. Consultants often start their careers as managers for a single campaign. If successful, they often hang out their shingles to give advice to campaigns. A consultant generally works within one political party, and provides guidance to as many as six or more different campaigns in an election season.

In the multi-million dollar campaign for an Illinois U.S. senator that I managed, I hired an experienced duo, who frequently worked as a team. One had been a PhD student of Henry Kissinger at Harvard, and was known for success in running campaigns for moderate Republican senatorial and gubernatorial candidates. The other was a veteran pollster, who directed surveys for, among others, the *Wall Street Journal*. These consultants and I wrote the campaign plan, with their input much more valuable than mine.

Some consultants have objectives possibly different from those of you and your candidate. They want/need to embellish their win-loss record to enhance their reputations, and thus their rates and future business. In this day of negative, attack advertising (which tends to work, unfortunately), consultants sometimes go "over the top" in their attacks on opponents. This can boomerang, reflect badly on you, and damage your own reputation. The candidate and his manager, not the consultants, are blamed for excesses.

You and your candidate must control the decisions of your campaign. For example, read all campaign messaging documents–advertising, brochures, social media communications–and approve them before they go out. I am aware of candidates who have signed–sight unseen–campaign messages that have resulted in defamation of character lawsuits.

I have also seen consultant billings to campaigns that have been wildly excessive, given the value of the work done. Managers should be clear at the outset what services they are contracting for, and insist on regular discussions about the work being done, so you have some sense of what you are getting for your money.

The campaign is over. You won. As Robert Redford wondered in the movie "The Candidate," on election night after winning: "What do I do now?"

Read on.

✳ CHAPTER 4 ✳

THE SUCCESSFUL LAWMAKER

As a newly elected state legislator, you should have developed a plan for what you want to achieve in your first term in office as well as for your overall goals for life in politics. The "game plan" should be based on your motivations in running for office. Do you have a cause or issue you want to champion? Do you see politics as an activity you wish to pursue as a career? Do you see your legislative path as a way to make a contribution to civic life and the world around you?

There are varied legislative roles you may seek to fulfill as part of your game plan. Societies have been assessing possible legislative roles at least since the Roman Republic. In 400-100 BC, the Roman Senate experimented with giving "the people" some—but not too much—increased representation via the office of *Tribune ex Populii* (Tribune of the People).[11] In the 1960s, when I was in graduate school, political scientist James David Barber observed the Connecticut legislature in action and determined several types of lawmaker: the *ritualist* (whom I might characterize as "the good ol' boy," who just liked being one of the gang); the *committee specialist* (subject matter expert); the *broker* (dealmaker); the *grandstander* (self-promoter), and the *lawmaker* (active in idea development and proposing of legislation).[12]

The point Barber makes is that each legislator tends by personality and energy to fill one or more of these roles, or variations on the theme. Each role makes a contribution to the process; even the ritualist fulfills the job of reflecting district values, or his own perspectives, simply by voting.

A part-time legislator can't fulfill every role effectively. There simply isn't enough time. The full-time legislator may become, say, both a lawmaking policymaker as well as a dealmaker, and even an expert over time, especially on a topic related to his outside career. I think it helpful when developing a game plan to examine oneself to determine the role(s) for which you are best suited. You can thus establish the types of achievement you might fulfill to the maximum, given personality and time available.

The new lawmaker should also be clear about what kind of representation he will provide his district. For example, the Eighteenth-Century English member of Parliament Edmund Burke became famous for his "Address to the Electors at Bristol" (his voters).[13] As was typical at the time, Burke did not live in the constituency he represented. He had voted in Parliament in support of free trade, which did not go down well with the many high-tariff business people in his district. To defend himself to his voters, Burke declared that he saw his higher responsibility in Parliament as that of a "trustee" of the national interest, and not solely the "agent" of his district, its voters and their wishes. I found in my experience as a state legislator, casting thousands of votes each biennial session, that I was a blend of the two, as are most lawmakers. The more important I sensed an issue was to my voters, the more weight I gave to serving as their agent. And yet there were also matters of principle to me, on which I had to vote my personal values, maybe as Burke felt he had to do.

There is also the role of leadership. Many candidates for office and elected officials trumpet their leadership qualities. I hate to disappoint you, but most legislators, certainly those who desire multiple terms in the legislature, are not leaders so much as they are followers. There is nothing wrong with this; it simply reflects the philosophy of trying to vote the way one's voters wish, even demand.

Yet I observe from my state of Illinois that the governors generally considered strong, courageous leaders were also one-term governors. A governor who espouses a tax increase, for example, whether warranted or not, frequently ends up out of office after one term. Leadership has its costs.

Become an expert in a subject. Legislatures need experts: on the budget; or a subject matter such as education, social services, the environment, economic development, even parliamentary procedure. Dealmaking, that is, the art of putting bi-partisan majorities together for legislation is another skill needed in a legislature and the Congress. Abraham Lincoln had to agree to some unsavory deals together in the U.S. House in 1865 to enact the 13th Amendment, which abolished slavery.[14]

Expertise is of great value to other members, and generates credits. You cannot be a respected expert in everything, yet over time you can develop deep knowledge of a major topic, such as the budget. Legislators will respect colleagues, even those from the other party, for their deeply informed subject matter counsel, often before turning to outside experts, staff and lobbyists.

Become the champion of an issue of importance to voters in your district. A former student of mine, who ran for the legislature in 2018, offers a good illustration: Merry Marwig's district lay in the path of new landing-and-takeoff patterns for scores of flights a day at O'Hare Airport. Deafening jet airplane noise bombarded her voters day and night. Merry energetically and publicly took on the authorities, to change patterns, and reduce noise. Though she didn't win her legislative race, Merry is still a champion to many in her community.

Be a helpmate to your fellow lawmakers whenever you can do so comfortably. And remember: little things mean a lot in a busy, reciprocity-oriented arena like a legislative body. For example, most bills die in committee. Yet, sometimes a fellow lawmaker has a strong need to see his bill receive a "Do Pass" majority in committee, so as to move it to the chamber floor. I heard a thousand times, it seems, a legislator proclaim in committee: "I have problems with this bill of my esteemed colleague, and I won't promise to vote for it on the House floor. Yet, I think so much of my colleague and the importance of the topic he is addressing with his bill, that I will vote Aye to help get this bill to the floor, where all house members may consider it."

This action generates a minor credit with the sponsor of the bill, who might return the favor on one of your bills. Yet there is cost to the process, that of sending too many bills to the House floor, where they clog the calendar and take inordinate time of the whole chamber. This is but one of many decisions a lawmaker makes daily during legislative sessions that may generate a return benefit. On balance, helping whenever one can is good politics, yet not necessarily good for the legislative process. Welcome to politics.

The successful legislator fulfills many tasks. By definition, the lawmaker proposes, evaluates, amends, passes-and-rejects thousands of bills each biennium. The lawmaker also has the important task of helping his constituents with their problems with government agencies. On important constituent and community problems, you will have to call an agency director, even the governor's office, or the governor himself, depending on the importance of the issue.

The effectiveness of these calls is often based upon the credits a lawmaker has built up with the respective players, and of the influence the lawmaker is seen to have within the legislature. In other words, a legislative leader from the governor's party gets his calls returned sooner than does a 'back bencher" from the other party. (In the House of Commons in the Parliament of the United Kingdom, the less important members sit high on the benches behind the party leaders, who are on the front bench.)

Lawmakers also serve as both advocates for and liaison between communities and economic interests in their districts with the executive branch of government. If a highway that provides critical service to a community is in bad repair, the lawmaker can seek repairs from the state DOT, or work in coalition with nearby lawmakers to seek reconstruction or new construction. Building coalitions among elected officials increase the clout they can bring to bear in seeking government action. The coalitions aggregate their influence within the legislature and in passing or defeating legislation important to the governor.

HOW TO PASS A BILL

As with your run for office, you have to develop a plan, to include strategy and tactics for passing your bill over opposition from interest groups, other legislators, maybe the governor, and possibly even the courts.

Everything important you want to achieve in politics takes longer than you expect, or so I have found, and every significant bill will have opposition. My major issue as a state House member decades ago was environmental, that of reclamation of land strip-mined for coal. Just because I thought reclamation of stripped land was an obviously terrific idea, didn't mean everyone else did. Understandably, the coal industry did not want to spend thousands of dollars extra per acre to regrade stripped land, which looked like the moonscape, into land that could over the years be farmed once again.

It took me two biennial sessions to pass a reclamation bill, and then a third session to amend the act into an even stronger piece of legislation (by then out of the legislature, I worked with a former colleague who saw the amendment through to enactment).[15]

The following will apply to your efforts to pass a bill.

Find experts who favor your idea, and who would later be willing to serve as credible witnesses before legislative committees. Your legislature may have staff who are experts on your issue, yet they may be prohibited from supporting your bill publicly.

Faculty at colleges, especially research-oriented universities, often have professors who might enjoy becoming involved in support of your policy idea. Unfortunately, for my reclamation idea, the agronomists I looked up at my state's land grant university were consultants to the coal industry!

I had no other experts available. In the 1960s, the Illinois Legislature provided nothing more than legal staff to put my idea into a bill. This alone would have been a disaster, as lawyers are not agronomists. (This has changed and most legislatures have competent researchers and experts available.)

So, lacking experts, I found an undergraduate student at a college in my district, who volunteered to do research for me on the complex topic of reshaping moonscapes into productive farmland, and of the costs of doing so. But obviously, the student lacked the background and knowledge to be a credible witness before a legislative committee skeptical of a first-term legislator's idea, especially an idea that had a phalanx of experts ready to testify as to why my bill was flawed. (The volunteer became a successful lawyer, and he and I are still good friends.)

EXPERTS ARE OFTEN NEEDED TO TESTIFY

Confirm in advance that the experts you drew upon earlier would be willing to testify in committee in support of your proposed legislation. Counsel them in advance to coordinate their testimony to avoid duplication. Ask for their understanding if time limits preclude their testimony, even though they may have traveled hours to be present. Tell them the key is to get the bill reported out of committee favorably, not to hear them testify. So, if it appears the bill is ready for a positive Do Pass vote, let the bill go forward, frustrating as that might be for people who came to the Capitol to testify. If this happens, you may owe your experts dinner that evening in the Capitol.

Develop good relationships with a veteran legislator or former legislator who can help you shape your strategy, based on his experience. In this regard, if one or more interest groups favor your idea, go to a lobbyist(s) who represents those groups for strategic and tactical ideas for your game plan.

Test out your policy idea among legislators, staff of your legislative leader and in the governor's office. Ask them to pick your idea apart, and help you put it back together. The best of these evaluators would be members and staff who are on the committee(s) that is likely to be assigned to hear your bill as introduced. All these players are busy with their own bills and responsibilities, so if they lack time, they may have ideas of others who could play this role.

Take your bill to the legislature's bill drafting agency. Sit down with the assigned bill drafter to discuss the bill at length, seeking his counsel as to the legal niceties of making your idea a legislative bill. Even though it's the bill drafter's job to assist you in making your idea a bill, be sure to show your understanding of how valuable you consider his expertise and assistance. You will need him or her and their colleagues in the future.

Build support for your bill. If there are interest groups that support you, they can obviously be critical at this stage. If there is little interest group support, yet significant potential support among the larger public, you may have to create your own "interest group" of folks who are committed to your idea.

For my strip-mining reclamation, I realized that farmers and county board members in counties affected by coal strip mining might favor my idea. That was also half a century ago, the earliest beginnings of environmental awakening, so many college students resonated with the idea. I recruited people from those worlds. We created a task force, raised a modest amount of money. We paid to fly key Illinois legislators to Ohio to tour strip-mining reclamation projects, to try to convince the lawmakers that cost-effective reclamation was practicable.

Get on the right committee. At the beginning of the legislative session, ask your legislative party leader to be assigned to the committee that is likely to hear your bill. This would depend on the importance of your bill to you, and of your other subject-matter interests, as well as the number of committees you might expect to serve on.

ROOKIE MISTAKES CAN BE COSTLY

The first step after introducing my reclamation bill was assignment to a committee. I didn't know politics was at play even at this early stage.

The Speaker of my House, as well as of my party, oversaw the assignment of bills. He could assign it to any committee he wished. The obvious committees were Mines & Minerals, Conservation, and Agriculture. The coal association had gone to him in advance of my even filing my legislation, to ask, successfully, that if such a bill were introduced that it be assigned to the Mines & Minerals Committee. The committee voted my bill Do Not Pass by a wide margin. Members of that committee had long been favorable to the coal industry, whereas the Agriculture Committee would have been more favorable to my bill. This is a good illustration of how a mentor lawmaker or former member can help you avoid rookie mistakes.

Have your supporters communicate with legislators. Find personal email addresses for legislators. Tell your supporters to make their communications brief, personal, with at least one specific reason for supporting your bill.

Since everyone communicates via social media, also have a number of personalized snail mail letters sent to legislators, with the same guidance as for the emails. Obviously, the more prominent and knowledgeable your communicators, the better. I was impressed as a young lawmaker that my seatmates on the House floor would often vote for or against a bill on the basis of just a single, or a few, personal, well-argued communications from voters in their districts, persons they had never met.

Count votes, in committee, and later on the floor. Don't take any member for granted. This is time consuming. You must go to each committee member individually. You may think certain members of your committee would like your proposal, or you might not have any idea. A committee member may already have committed to opponents to vote against your bill in committee. Other committee members may not know anything about your idea and its good points, so you will have to educate each such member. Know in advance what the outcome will be. And don't expect passionate speeches in committee and on the floor to carry the day; generally, they don't.

Each legislative chamber has its own rules, procedures, and rituals. And each piece of legislation has its own unique quirks and needs, not all of which can be covered here. You must shepherd your bill every step along the tortuous path from drafting to signature by the chief executive.

The successful lawmaker wears many hats. Your overarching responsibility is to assess what will improve and strengthen your district and make life better for your voters. This requires listening to voters, via town hall meetings and radio call-in shows. The effective lawmaker also works with colleagues to enhance the vitality of the larger city, state, and nation he represents. It's a big task, yet legislative service can be rewarding and satisfying.

★ CHAPTER 5 ★

THE EFFECTIVE LEGISLATIVE STAFFER

Behind every successful lawmaker is likely to be an effective legislative staff. Today, legislators in medium-size and large states often have several assistants, and even a top staffer called "chief of staff." A member of the U.S. House has 15 or more assistants. The effective legislative staffer can extend his boss's reach and effectiveness significantly.

The "staffer" to a lawmaker is one of the most important roles in government, which few citizens know exists. The position has developed, beginning in the 1960s, as state legislatures, Congress and big city governments "modernized," that is, increased their capacities to serve constituents (and, I should note, enhance incumbent re-election chances).

The legislative staffer is usually a young person, and often one who came over from an election campaign role. When I entered the Illinois Legislature half a century ago, there were no legislative staffers, not even offices from which to work. Then came secretaries for legislators, who quickly learned to handle matters for their bosses that went beyond taking transcription and sending out letters; in effect, they became administrative assistants. The roles of the staffer are as varied as the respective needs of each lawmaker.

Each assistant/lawmaker relationship is unique, so I must generalize. The tasks may include scheduling, speech writing, policy research, travel around the district to meet with constituents, and representation of your boss at meetings and, of course, handling constituent inquiries. Staffers are important because they do most of the problem-solving for constituents.

They also serve as the eyes and ears of their bosses, as to the mood and pulse of what is going on in the district.

Constituents come to elected officials with myriad problems. Typical of those that fall in the lap of the legislative staffer include: driver and vehicle issues; state benefits, including unemployment and Medicaid matters, and tax questions for the state revenue department. Tougher "asks" from constituents might involve, for example, trying to get a state prison inmate transferred to a prison closer to the inmate's family; or resolving a dispute between a mother and the state child welfare agency over a youngster who has been removed from the mother's care, or checking out why a family has been cut off from social services benefits.

The two most important words for the legislative assistant (and for all people in politics) are: "Thank You." Here is but one important illustration of why these words are so valuable. The list of constituent problems is long. A medium-size state government might have 40 agencies on its organization chart. The federal government is an order of magnitude even more complex and unfathomable than our state governments. That is why legislative staff are critical in navigating governments for constituents.

Government agency staff are generally decent, capable people. And most significant agencies have staff assigned to be liaison between the agency and elected officials. Their job is to be helpful when they can, as good relations with lawmakers, who approve agency budgets, make all the sense in the world.

On the other hand, these liaisons also exist to protect their agencies. So, if your lawmaker has a beef with an agency, and wants you to probe into the agency's workings, the liaison is likely to be resistant to your inquiries. This will be the case especially if this staff person has a less than positive view of you. So, developing good relationships with agency personnel is critical. Even "Thank You" can go a long way. If a bureaucrat bends over backwards to help you with a constituent's problem, a note from your lawmaker to the boss of the agency liaison can go a long way in developing good relationships.

If you (the legislative staffer) are stuck in a remote district office, or mostly working from home, ask your lawmaker boss for the okay to travel to the state capitol or D.C. for a day or two, for purposes of making the rounds of the people with whom you are talking with frequently on the phone. Get to know as many agency people as possible. It is helpful to tie name to face (and personality), and for the opportunity to ask questions of the agency person(s) about how to interact most effectively–people love to be asked for their expert guidance.

As for the constituents who call to ask for your assistance, take their problem(s) seriously, even if they don't seem so important to you. After all, the constituent wouldn't have taken the step to call you if she hadn't thought the matter important. People who contact your office don't always expect you to solve their problems. You are often their last, best hope. So, if you convey the sense that you are working hard on their behalf, they will develop a positive view of you–and thus your boss–even if their problem remains a problem.

Often a constituent comes to your office without knowing whether her problem is a state or federal government issue. For example, the state-based legislative staffer may receive a call about a Social Security issue, which is obviously a federal rather than state matter. So, you call your counterpart in the office of the local U.S. congressman. Here again, developing good relations is critical. You two–state and federal legislative staffers–need one another, as problems often cross governmental boundaries.

FROM LEGISLATIVE STAFF TO U.S. SECRETARY OF TRANSPORTATION

The role of legislative staffer has become a route into elective office for young people who aspire to elective office. As illustration: My friend Ray LaHood began as a school teacher in central Illinois; then worked in a local delinquency prevention program; was appointed to fill an unexpired term in the state legislature; and lost his race for the seat. He then became legislative staff assistant to a congressman, and moved up to chief of staff to the congressman.

When his boss retired, Ray ran for that seat in Congress, was elected, and served 14 years (1995-2009) as a Republican. He had a fascinating career in Congress. For example, in 1998, House Speaker Newt Gingrich asked Ray to preside over the House of Representative hearings that resulted in the impeachment of President Bill Clinton. This, because Ray had developed deep knowledge of parliamentary procedure. In 2009, Democrat President Barack Obama appointed his fellow Illinoisan LaHood to become Secretary of Transportation (2009-2013). Quite a career for a legislative staffer, and far from unique.[16]

If your constituent's problem(s) involve another government, don't simply tell the constituent to call that government agency; this really frustrates a voter who has likely already been bounced around. *You* make the contact with the congressman's office, pass along the constituent's problem(s). Report back to your constituent what you have done, what the constituent might expect from the other office, and if possible, about when would you and the constituent can expect to hear back. Remember: good government is good politics, that is, your constituent will value your efforts (and thus your boss) if you see his or her problem through to the end.

Always make every effort to keep elective politics out of the office. This is almost impossible, of course, as the two worlds are intertwined. But, no fundraising, no discussion of campaigning in the office. Some legislative staff aspire to careers in politics. The best way to prepare for such is simply to do the most effective job possible for your boss, without ever feathering your own nest via your boss's good offices. Of course, during all this time you are absorbing valuable perspectives about people, government processes and public policy.

★ CHAPTER 6 ★

GOVERNMENT MANAGEMENT: PRACTICAL GUIDANCE FOR NEW AGENCY DIRECTORS

The end game of politics is for the winners to govern. Politics and government are inseparable. Much of governing is done by agency directors (heads, managers) on behalf of their chief executives.

Walter Bagehot was a brilliant 19th Century English journalist who edited *The Economist*, an English magazine that is still well read today. Bagehot observed that, "The job of a minister is not to run his ministry, but to see that it runs well." (A minister in the United Kingdom is the member of Parliament appointed to oversee a major government agency [ministry].) Bagehot's sage advice applies well to those who direct major agencies of both national and state governments in the United States.

Agency heads are in some jurisdictions political appointees; in others, longtime government administrators. Even the latter are involved in politics, as the political world of chief executives, legislators, interest groups and even the media want to tell the agency heads how to do their jobs. Sitting or former legislators are sometimes appointed to head state agencies. The lawmaker cum director brings valuable political skills to his or her new job, but often needs to learn additional competencies.

Over the decades, I worked for three Illinois governors (from 1960-2009, four of the seven Illinois governors were imprisoned; I worked for the other three). Several times, my governors asked me to serve as interim director of different state agencies. The directive from the governor, for these

39

roughly half-year assignments, was "to fix" the troubled agencies, which I never accomplished. But I learned that state agencies are important, often complex. For example, a state department of children's services is assigned the daunting task of rebuilding the lives of thousands of children damaged by neglect and often violent abuse. These youngsters are wards of the state, that is, of you and me as citizen taxpayers.

Let's say that Joseph ("Just call me Joe") Blowhard has just been elected governor. He has to fill out a cabinet of 20 agency directors. Because as a legislator you developed an expertise in the environment and natural resources, Gov. Joe has nominated you to be director of the state department of natural resources. You are to serve on an interim basis until–and if–you are confirmed by your state senate.

After your first day at the director's big desk, the first thing that hits you is how many people want to "help" you run your agency. These include the governor's staff, legislators, legislative staff, the governor's budget office, myriad interest groups (whose objectives are often in conflict with one another), lobbyists, local community groups that want a new state park, your federal government "sister" agency, and the natural resources reporters– if there are any left–at your state's major newspapers, among others.

In other words, you are embedded in a sticky web of government and politics (see graphic nearby).

The Web of Government

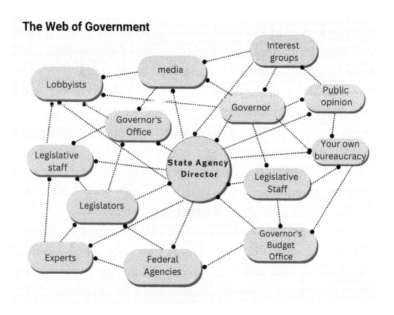

YOU AND YOUR AGENCY

You are the new kid on the block, and you will likely be viewed that way for all of your tenure as director. Agency employees were there long before you, and will be there long after. You may think, as director, that you are in charge. Yet you will only be effective if you make it clear, and later a fact, that you want to be, with them, an important part of their team. If you are a former legislator, not improbable, you can offer to bring to the table your experience and relationships with lawmakers as a resource for the agency team of top staffers and division managers.

Be visible around your agency. Management by walking around can be a morale builder with agency employees, whether you have a total of 100 or 20,000. The bureaucracy is filled with decent, capable people who often believe deeply in the mission of their agency.

Get to know the rules, the administrative rules, this is. Legislation is often passed with lots of ambiguity. This allows lawmakers to avoid detail in their bills that might create opposition from some quarters. Thus, they leave details, often important ones, to be sorted out via the creation of administrative rules, which are necessary for agency heads to implement the legislation.

This has often been the case with environmental legislation. The legislation might say, rather vaguely, "There shall be clean air," and then leave it up to the state EPA to promulgate rules that define what specifically is meant by "clean air"—how clean, and how achieved?! Agency rules can run to hundreds of pages; these rules might limit the actions you would otherwise wish to take, or they might give the agency director great latitude. Either read the rules yourself, or receive detailed briefings as to what rules you must follow.

Don't accept "The agency can't do that." The power of agency employees is largely passive, not active. It consists of the capacity to withhold needed services and information, rather than in the capacity to oppose political superiors directly. "I'm sorry, Director, but we can't do that." Of course, your ability to get done the things that "can't be done" is one of the biggest assets you as agency director can bring to the governor.

One way to build this capacity is to develop confidence among your team that you are working hard *with* them, and to show appreciation for their contributions to the agency.

Whenever possible, brag up the agency and its employees to the outside world. Your executive team and agency employees will appreciate you deeply.

Work closely with the extended office of the governor. Surrounding the governor are several, generally young "hot shots," who can be helpful to you, or not. Most important of these are the governor's deputy (or comparable title) who has you and your agency in his or her portfolio of responsibilities. This deputy is the primary contact between you and the governor. Don't try to run around this staffer unless absolutely necessary. The governor has assigned the deputy as your liaison, so must have some confidence in this key staff member. Try to develop good relationships with the deputy.

Possibly even more important than the governor's deputy, is the analyst in the Governor's Office of Management and Budget who is assigned to analyze the budget needs—what can be more important—of your agency.

"HAVE YOU SEEN YOUR ANALYST THIS RECENTLY?"

I had volunteered in the campaign of a gubernatorial candidate. Upon his election, I was asked to stay on in a professional role in his transition into office; my subject matter was education, about which I knew something. The budget office analyst for education and I were to be a duo in briefing the governor-elect on this topic. It became clear to all of us early on in the transition that the budget analyst was far more important to the transition than I was. I recall the frustrated lament of the incoming governor, who loved to spend money: "Okay," as he looked pointedly at the budget analyst, "how much *can't* I spend today?" The budget analyst for your agency is key, and you should see this person regularly.

Hold regular, collaborative meetings with your top agency staff. The governor's office and your agency's top people may have differing objectives and agendas. Your challenge is, where necessary, to referee and mediate/arbitrate as best you can, as you really represent both the governor's office and the agency.

Find middle ground wherever possible when in conflict with members of the Legislature. The Legislature often wants to tell you how to run your agency, and members may have had negative run-ins with agency staff over the years. Again, in such situations, finding middle ground where possible is a role the agency director needs to play. Your agency probably has a staffer assigned to be the "legislative liaison." This person is the day-to-day go-between your agency and legislators. If you are not able to name your own legislative liaison for the agency, you should work hard to develop a good working relationship with this staffer. This liaison also helps solve problems that constituents bring to their legislators. In addition, this staffer assists you and the governor's office in achieving goals you have set for the agency.

Keep legislative leaders or their staff informed of agency activities. As agency director, you and your legislative liaison should develop good relationships, as possible, with the legislative leaders of both parties in both chambers of the legislature. Courtesy calls and periodic follow-up to the leaders, or their staff, as your legislative liaison feels appropriate, is generally useful. Make calls as well to the top budget committee chairs and minority spokesmen to discuss your agency's budget situation and needs makes sense.

THERE IS NO ONE TO BROOD ABOUT
THE PROBLEMS OF THE FUTURE

Decades ago, North Carolina governor Terry Sanford lamented that, "There is no one in the governor's office whose only job is to gaze out the window and brood about the problems of the future."[17] That's still true today. So, maybe you, your agency team and others in your "web" could fulfill that role, at least within the context of your agency and its mission.

This might be an exercise in thinking about what you all want the agency to achieve five years out. After all, you can't get anywhere unless you know where you're going. Involve as many people from the larger web as possible, as they all want to be in the loop. Establish a dashboard of measurable indicators of agency success, and review them regularly with your team.

On the other hand, I add quickly, maybe your agency is up to its eyeballs in alligators in an unhealthy swamp, leaving no time for long-term thinking. In other words, each agency is unique.

As director you are largely the liaison between your agency, the governor's office and the web of government in which you are entangled. You are Mr. Outside, while your team within the agency directs inside operations. Whether it is a governor's administration or the White House, the agency head's role is basically the same. Developing and leading a good, effective team is the most critical task of an effective director.

CHAPTER 7

EVERYBODY'S A LOBBYIST!

Lobbying is an honorable profession, integral to the political process, even though the outside world may have a rather negative opinion of lobbyists. Lobbying is the practice of directly petitioning our government and its elected and appointed officials (as our US Constitution gives us the right to do), in order to achieve a goal(s) set by your employer or client. "Governmental relations" is the broader term for setting and achieving the strategies and goals of a company, union, or association. Many lobbyists participate in and inform this strategy setting.

The term lobbyist derives from England in the 1640s. The public could meet and talk with members of Parliament in the lobby of the House of Commons.[18] I estimate roughly that there are more than 100,000 professional, compensated lobbyists in the U.S.--12,000 registered in the nation's Capital; about 50,000 total in our state capitals, and maybe 25,000 or more working the halls (and lobbies) of our big city governments.

Everyone is a lobbyist, you might say, as an advocate. Whether trying to convince one's love to the altar; or a boss that you deserve a raise, or that an increase in the minimum wage is a terrific (or terrible) idea.

I was a terrible lobbyist. The game is not for everyone. For several years in the 1990s, I was president of a respected statewide business trade association in Illinois. Lobbying was part of the job. Given my PhD and background in college teaching, I tended then–and now–to see the world "on the one hand; on the other hand…" Not so in lobbying, which is almost pure advocacy. You're a salesman. Your job is to convince lawmakers and decision makers of the absolute rightness of your client's position. I was thus terribly uncomfortable as a lobbyist. I lasted a few years, then departed the job when I felt it wouldn't be embarrassing to do so, for either me or my employer.

Most lobbyists are employees of a company, union and nonprofit organization, and their jobs are titled "government relations." Then, there is the "hired gun," a lobbyist who works under contract, generally for more than one client. She or he is valuable for strategic and tactical thinking skills and experience in the political arena, and because the hired gun may have special relationships with key lawmakers. This lobbyist may not have nor need an intimate grasp of the issues, although it helps. After all, she can bring that expertise along, as necessary, yet the expert may not be available at the moment you need her.

The hired gun loves the game, and the money, which can be very good. A salary and bonus of $100,000-150,000 is a typical range, with top contract lobbyists earning multiples of that. Satisfaction also comes from achieving her assignment, whether killing a bill, or passing a bill, the latter being much more difficult than the former. Or maybe her assignment is to convince an agency executive or the governor's office to soften or create a rule that benefits her client.

Over the past half century, the number of lobbyists has increased significantly. The expansion of governments has, for example, increased the number of nonprofit organizations and local governments that have either their own lobbyist or engage a contract lobbyist to look after their interests. There has been, over time, a decline in the number of lawyer lobbyists and an attendant increase in the number who have poli sci and communications degrees.

GET TO KNOW YOUR ARENA

An internship in one or both the executive and legislative branches of a political arena offers good preparation for plying the trade of lobbying. Campaign experience is also valuable; walk in the shoes of a candidate out on the hustings. This will help you see politics from several dimensions. During that time, hone your skills at understanding the web of government.

Whether as intern or junior lobbyist, you need to grasp each official's unique needs, interests, biases, goals and objectives. That is, what makes the lawmaker tick, what rings his bell. "Needs" is a complex term as used here.

Each legislator has his own underlying personal, psychological, economic "needs" to fulfill. These can include status, respect, appreciation for his intelligence, proof of his skills in passing bills or achieving compromise, willingness to trade credits for debits, and others.

Don't assume anything in advance about a lawmaker. Even the most conservative lawmaker might have a soft spot for arts and culture, and be willing to support such, even though he is dead-set against spending otherwise. This makeup of the lawmaker may affect his willingness–or not–to help you get a bill out of committee, even if he will oppose your bill vigorously on the floor. Another legislator may see your bill of the moment as sound logically, yet be committed to another lobbyist to oppose it. Another legislator may not like your bill, but may see a favorable vote on the bill as a way to gain favor with the chief sponsor of the bill, whose support he needs on an issue important to the legislator.

THE LOBBYING GAME IS IN TRANSITION

Technology and the 2020-2022 pandemic have wrought major changes in the lobbying process. Lobbying has always been about sociability and communications. If you don't enjoy being with people in social settings, you probably won't fit into the lobbying game. You don't have to love the subject matter on which you are lobbying, but you need to enjoy the process, the strategy setting, the chess game of politics.

Socializing used to take place largely at restaurant dinners, with lobbyists picking up the tab. Half a century ago, the primary purpose of the dinners was relationship building, critical to the long-term success of a lobbyist. Rarely were specific pieces of legislation mentioned, at least not in my experience. In recent years, however, many states have imposed rules that require public disclosure of payment for these dinners. Some candidates are thus able to play "gotcha," by publicizing and criticizing these private dinners. As a result, much socializing is now focused on candidate fundraisers.

As Joan Parker, a former Speaker of the Third House in Illinois (the lobbyists' informal association), observes: "It is hard to talk about lobbying without talking about PACs (political action committees) and fundraising. No serious lobbyist in Illinois can avoid fundraisers if she or he wants to be successful."[19] Contributions to lawmakers by lobbyists, generally courtesy of their clients, are obviously important to the role a lobbyist can play, at least in my Illinois. For example, the trade group for which I lobbied was not organized to make campaign contributions. This generally limited my group's influence to the front end of the public policy process, when our expert information was valuable in helping shape complicated legislation.

My organization rarely played a role at the end of the legislative process, in hammering out the "big bills" in the back rooms of the capitol. These bills were often important to major businesses and unions, or where big money was being spent by lobbyists, such as gambling legislation. Lobbyists who benefit from well-funded PACs are, maybe unfortunately, likely to be "players" during the bargaining over the big money bills. After all, much of politics and public policy is about money, that is, who gets what.

The pandemic changed, maybe into the future, how lobbyists and lawmakers communicate. Zoom and remote platforms have replaced some of the in-person communications and relationship building that are so valuable to lobbyists. Lawmakers tend to like remoteness, which reduces travel to the capitol, as well as interaction with lobbyists to whom they might have to say No, even when they have earlier taken their campaign contributions. Expect Zoom to replace some or much of the old-style ability to interact.

On the other hand, the smartphone has made communications easier for lobbyists. A lobbyist can sit in a committee hearing room or a legislative chamber gallery and text back and forth with a lawmaker(s) in real time. The lobbyists can provide guidance and useful information to a lawmaker on the floor during debate.

☆ ☆ ☆

In politics, there are no permanent enemies, and no permanent friends, only permanent interests—original author unknown; legions take credit for the saying

TIPS FOR THE NEW LOBBYIST

I used to tell my students that a good lobbyist provides the right information, in the right format, to the right people, at the right time. I still think that is a good summary. To be effective at these tasks, the following tips are important:

"Be around" and be helpful. Be around the process, the places where lobbyists and lawmakers gather. In Illinois, there is a brass rail that encircles the opening under the Capitol dome, located between the third-floor doors to the House and Senate chambers. "Polishing the rail" (leaning against the rail) is a hallowed tradition for many lobbyists and lawmakers. This is a gathering place when folks are at ease, ready to barter intelligence about what is going on that day, and what is on order for the next.

Get to know people. Introduce yourself to people in the game who went to your college. Join informal groups. Introduce yourself to just about anyone you possibly can. This is a people game. You're a part of it now, and lobbyists will appreciate you for it. Everyone is sucking in information at all times, even from you. Go around and introduce yourself at the offices of legislators and their pertinent staff, agency people, other lobbyists, newspaper reporters (what few there are left), and, especially, to the administrative assistants for all the above.

Administrative assistants are often the gatekeepers to their bosses, and they are full of information about the process and what is happening when. Also get to know the people for whom you work, not just your boss, but people in the company or association from whom you can also learn, e.g. especially the experts on the subject matter. After all, you will be needing the help of all these people at one time or another.

Find a mentor. Try to develop a relationship with an experienced lobbyist. He or she might be willing, over a beer after a session day, to give you their counsel, respond to your questions about what was really going on that day, and offer some tips about how to play the game. Of course, this person may be your boss, but your senior may be too busy for such. You are going through an apprenticeship, and you need counsel from experienced hands.

Ask questions. People generally love to talk about what they do, if they are at ease. If you ask them questions, they think you must feel they are important. Then, listen. Listening is generally more important than talking.

Don't hold grudges. As the old saying in politics goes: There are no permanent enemies, and no permanent friends, only permanent interests.

Never lie, and tell the whole story. Your word is your bond. Bills are often complicated. You must inform the lawmaker of all the pieces of the bill that might conceivably affect him and his constituents. When working to convince a lawmaker to side with your client's position, you must also apprise the lawmaker of who—other lawmakers, interest groups, citizen groups—will be on the other side of this issue, and how strongly so.

One lobbyist goes even further in explaining how he plied his trade: "From time to time, not too often, of course, I tell a lawmaker important to me to "vote his district" and against my association's position." That is real relationship building.

"ROSTY" REPAYS A FAVOR

Being helpful pays off. I have a friend who, for many years, was the chief lobbyist for the Illinois Medical Society, the important doctors' lobby. My friend lived at the northern tip of Illinois, not far from upscale Lake Geneva, Wisconsin. That is where U.S. Rep. Dan Rostenkowski had a weekend place, a retreat for golf and dinner with his buddies. At the time, "Rosty" was one of the most important people in D.C., as chair of the House Ways & Means Committee.

My friend Don was a golfer, and once Rosty needed another golfer at the last minute. Somehow Don was available and glad to fill in, which he did. After that, whenever the congressman needed a golfer, Don was sure to be available. And Don would help Rosty set up and serve the drinks. It was fun.

Then one week, Don and other state medical lobbyists were called to Washington by their national counterpart organization on a critical lobbying matter. Their problem: The national leaders couldn't get to the aloof Rostenkowski, not even to his chief of staff, both of whom held the keys to success, or not, for the doctors. The national group was desperate.

So, Don called Rostenkowski's secretary, explained his relationship with "the Chairman." Not ten minutes later, Don received a call back, with an appointment for his crew to see Rostenkowski later that day.

You never know when help you have provided someone in the political fraternity will pay off.

Talk the lawmaker's language. The people lobbyists deal with consider themselves busy, and are sometimes under great stress, certainly so near the end of a legislative session. Lobbyists need to know how much information lawmakers need to know about your issues, and how they want to learn it. You have to learn how to communicate your pitch succinctly, or more expansively, depending on the legislator. Some lawmakers simply want a one sentence explanation of how the bill affects voters in their districts; others, more information about the pros and cons, while the few legislative specialists in your subject matter will want a detailed briefing.

Don't promise more than you can produce. As more than one lobbyist has told me: "One of the most important jobs is that of educating your client or employer as to what is possible–or not–in the political arena. In any legislative session, the lobbyist and her client might be able to get a couple of slices of the loaf of bread, but rarely the whole loaf."

Get your client's people involved in their issues. When you have moved up to the role of chief lobbyist for an association, union or company, you are now responsible for helping set the lobbying goals and the strategies by which to achieve them.

Encourage your client's top people to become active in the political process, to the extent they have the time and interest. For example, back to my friend, Don, the medical society lobbyist. One of his doctors, a heart surgeon, saved the life of powerful Chicago Mayor Richard J. Daley following a heart attack. The mayor told the surgeon he was grateful and would do anything for him. Later, the doctor offered to help Don get a treasured appointment with Daley, at which they asked for his help. Democratic Boss Daley agreed to support the surgeon and the medical society, as a personal favor, in moving a key piece of legislation–that the Mayor's own party leadership had stalled!

If you think you might enjoy "football without muscles," you might well make a good lobbyist.

★ CHAPTER 8 ★

CORRUPTION: I DIDN'T PLAN TO BE UNETHICAL

Corruption is an especially important topic to me, because I have been so close to it. Three of my college apartment-mates were later "measured for striped suits," that is, sent to prison, one for political corruption, and two for crimes in their professional lives. As college students, two of the three were active in church work; one actually served as lay minister to a rural church that lacked a minister.

Why then, years later, would these good fellows abuse either the trust of their colleagues, or the legal rules of the game? Probably the hubris of very smart men, and possibly because they never gave their actions a thought. Thinking about ethics doesn't take a lot of brainpower, but you do have to keep some basic thoughts on the desktop screen of your mind.

Few people enter elected office planning to be unethical. Before leaving office, however, many public officials appear to have acted unethically at some time, at least in the eyes of opponents, editors, courts of law, and maybe even worse, friends and family. Painful, crushing costs of politics and government are always lurking.

Between 1985 and 2020, 57,000 persons were indicted in the U.S. for public corruption, from the local to the national level, and three-quarters were convicted of their crimes, often for participating in bribery.[20] If you become involved in politics and government, always keep in the back of your mind: How do I want to be remembered by my friends, my children?

When I was first elected to the Illinois House of Representatives in 1968 as an innocent 26-year-old, a fellow freshman gave each of his new colleagues a copy of Robert Bolt's play, *A Man for All Seasons*.[21] This popular work is about Chancellor Thomas More's unwillingness to capitulate, on principle, to Henry the VIII's demands for a divorce, for which the churchman paid the price with his head.

I was thunderstruck. As in Thomas More's England, there were matters of principle and ethics in the venture I was embarking upon! I simply had never thought about it. I am still indebted to the late U.S. Rep. George O'Brien for that precious gift of awakening.

HOW DO YOU WANT TO BE REMEMBERED?

A number of my colleagues in the Illinois House were "sent up the river" in the 1970s for taking just a few hundred bucks each in return for voting to approve heavier weight limits for cement trucks. This was maybe small beer to the lawmakers in that era, but it became big to federal prosecutors.

Years later, when I was teaching at the University of Illinois, a student entered my office, hesitantly. He was handsome, the spitting image of one of those lawmaker lawbreakers, a fellow who died in prison, a broken man.

Awkwardly, the student began: "I'm told you knew my father. I was just a baby when he got in trouble, so I never really knew him. What was he like?"

"He was a man of goodwill, liked by his colleagues," I said. "He simply went along with the guys, and didn't think about what he was doing." It was a difficult conversation.

This matter of ethics became personal during a public flap in the 1990s over valuable tuition-free scholarships to Illinois public universities. Then (no longer), each member of the Illinois General Assembly awarded two four-year, free-ride scholarships to whomever. While most of these General Assembly Scholarships went to highly deserving students, sometimes they went, quietly, to the children of relatives, political friends, and even other legislators. During the flap, I had responded to a reporter with a holier-than-thou observation that most of us legislators proved able to resist such pressures.

Just one week after making that remark, I was at a dinner party in my legislative district. Oblivious to the controversy and my comment, an old friend reminisced about how she had once defended me in her community when it became known that I had awarded a legislative scholarship, a generation earlier, to the son of a prominent family in my district. Ouch.

I vaguely recalled the situation. The family had made a good case that the son had been unfairly denied admission to the University of Illinois, and the legislative scholarship would provide not only free tuition but also assure admission. Maybe I was too easily convinced. No big deal in the larger scheme of things, yet my friend had felt a need to come to my defense, all unknown to me. Double ouch.

What constitutes unethical behavior in politics? I define political corruption as anything of unearned personal gain at public expense. There is both illegal corruption as well as legal corruption. Maybe my scholarship award, worth thousands of dollars, was legal corruption. I did not gain personally, although maybe later, I can't remember, the prominent family contributed significantly to a political campaign of mine, as a kind of thank you.

The public has little trust and confidence in public officials. In 1970, during my first term in the Illinois House of Representatives, a colorful Illinois politician died unexpectedly, leaving nearly a million dollars ($6 million in 2023 dollars) stuffed in shoe boxes in his state capital hotel room. For months after, friends and acquaintances in my district would accost me, chuckling, with queries about where my shoe boxes were located. I was shaken by their tone, because I sensed they felt I might indeed have "shoe boxes" hidden somewhere, or that someday I would succumb to the seductions of illicit politics.

People enter politics rather blindly. If they give any thought in advance to right and wrong in politics, they assume the distinctions are clear, like black and white. But politics is cast largely in grey hues. Might an elected official do wrong while thinking he is doing good for the student of a prominent family? I think there are several reasons that elected officials become snarled in the net of public criticism for actual or apparent unethical behavior:

"This is the way it's always been done." The legislative scholarship program was a century old, and for decades many legislators viewed the scholarships as one of their few perquisites of office.

Changing ethical standards. What might have been acceptable two generations ago, had it even been reported, might not be today.

Cultural tolerance. In some local political cultures in Illinois, a lawmaker would be criticized for *failing* to help her friend or supporter with a scholarship, regardless of merit.

The psychological and career pressures to win election and re-election. People who run the gauntlet of a campaign for office want to win, badly. And for state legislators and congresspeople who are developing careers in politics, re-election is so important that their thinking about the ethics of decisions can become skewed, clouded, or blocked out by more pressing matters.

"I seen my opportunities and I took 'em," as Boss Plunkitt of old Tammany Hall reportedly bragged. We cannot ignore the role of greed and rationalization, the latter justifying the former, though I think avarice is much less significant than are the pressures to win re-election.

So, I offer **"Nowlan's Practical Guide to Ethical Decision Making"**:

Think! Is there any dimension of a decision that could be seen by others to represent personal benefit at public expense, even indirectly? As a savvy political friend mused, "How would this decision be viewed by a grand jury?"

Never justify a decision on the basis that "this is the way it has always been done." Time and attitudes change.

Identify a friend or acquaintance whom you respect for integrity. This person would serve as your "second-opinion conscience." How would your friend regard a tentative decision, one that could have ethical dimensions?

How do you want your children to remember you? Could this decision conceivably hurt them or diminish you in their eyes, even years later?

Melodramatic? I don't think so. After all, if only those officials who planned to be unethical actually were, the issue of ethics would not so frequently blanket the news in Illinois and across the nation.

CHAPTER 9

IS THERE A FUTURE FOR YOU IN POLITICS AND GOVERNMENT?

This "starter kit" is a primer about "how to do" politics and government, not about "what to do" in government, which is another book(s). I conclude this basic work by briefly reprising a few important themes and discussing with you the question of "whether" you should somehow get involved.

Politics and government are inseparable: the first leads to the second, and there is overlap across the two in the struggle for power and influence. Nothing wrong with that. After all, as Mayor Richard Daley of Chicago said: "Good government is good politics." To the extent possible, we should prevent people from using government to further political ends. Your job in politics and government is *public* service, not *personal* service.

> Your work in politics and government is *public* service, not *personal* service.

If you do at some point jump into the fray of politics, appreciate that winning, while always the goal, is not the only benefit from running. As a young 24-year-old, I ran for the Illinois House, and lost, narrowly. But I learned how to run, and two years later, I was elected. The second and winning race was really an extension of the first, losing race. During his political career from the 1830s to his assassination in 1865, Abraham Lincoln lost six election contests and won nine.[22] In losing, a candidate may be able to give greater voice to a cause he or she espouses, and may advance the ultimate achievement of his objectives, even in losing.

Politics is, as Moley observed in the first chapter, "a condition of life, like the atmosphere we breathe." At its best, politics is a noble pursuit, the quest for what I consider the never-ending search for order, harmony and prosperity in our tumultuous society. Government also serves the fundamental purpose of resolving conflict. If there were no conflict among us, there would be little reason for legislative bodies.

I have found that government can ameliorate people problems, but at great cost. We are spending ever-more taxpayer money in laudable efforts to make life better for all. To do so, however, government keeps expanding. All government spending in 2022, during the pandemic, approached half of total Gross Domestic Product, before falling back to 38 percent in 2024. I am not opposed to spending, if done effectively. There must be a point, however, when government spending will turn the trajectory of wealth creation from upward to downward. Wealth determines our capacity to address problems through government. I pose this not to answer the question, yet to illustrate one of the thorny problems participants in politics and government wrestle with continually.

There are significant rewards to be earned, as well as possible costs, from entering public life. You can derive immense personal satisfaction from serving one's community, state and nation. You can also add to the well-being of society, and gain the respect of those around you.

Lawyers help clients, and in doing so generally make *private* policy, that is, resolve conflict for individuals and small groups. Yet, few people in our nation are accorded the privilege of making *public* policy, that is, the laws, rules and outcomes that affect society generally.

Although I never achieved the highest tier of political office and public service, I have taken great satisfaction in legislative achievements and in planting policy ideas that others carried forward. I also had success in electing into top offices those I respected. I also made lifelong friendships among politicians of both major parties, as we all suffered the same slings and arrows of campaigning and of jousting with one another in our legislative politics.

The following advice is fitting in every chapter of this starter kit, especially when one is contemplating activity in politics. You may know it, from Shakespeare's *Hamlet*, as Polonius' counsel to his son, who is heading off to university: "This above all: to thine own self be true, And it must follow, as the night the day, thou canst not then be false to any man."

The ancient Romans put great stock in what they called virtue (*virtus*). This term encompassed courage, integrity, honor, steadfastness, service before ambition, and more.[23] The transition from the republican form of government to dictatorial emperors in ancient Rome is often attributed, at least in part, to the decline in virtue among their political leaders, to putting ambition before service.

Who better than Founder Benjamin Franklin to quote, in closing. There is a story, often told, that upon exiting the Constitutional Convention, Benjamin Franklin was approached by a group of citizens who asked what sort of government the delegates had created. His answer was: "A republic, if you can keep it."[24] That continues to be the fundamental calling of politics and public service. Virtue: Embody it. Politics depends upon it.

So, participate, whether in helping others gain a foothold in politics; in running for office; in service inside government in executive, policy and expert roles, and in enlivening the public discourse via debate and opinion writing.

Help us keep this Republic.

FOR FURTHER READING

Politics is about people, so I recommend a few of my favorite books from history about those who played the game of politics with passion and skill. By the way, these politicians, most of whom became president, started out as local government officials and state legislators. I list the figures in historical order.

The Prince, Niccolò Machiavelli. The 16th Century Italian author has given his name to practical politics. In this work, Machiavelli provides brutally practical guidance for those who would lead his city-state of Florence.

Team of Rivals: The Political Genius of Abraham Lincoln, Doris Kearns Goodwin. Thousands of books have been turned out about Lincoln. This is one of the best. The work displays Lincoln's brilliance in gathering in, managing, drawing upon, and leading his Cabinet of strong, cantankerous, yet ultimately admiring rivals, all during the darkest days of our Civil War.

Huey Long, T. Harry Williams. An unsophisticated yet wily, populist force of nature, Long mesmerized the poorer classes of Louisiana and served as both governor and U.S. senator in the 1920-30s—simultaneously! President Franklin Roosevelt worried that Long might unseat him, but an assassin intervened to snuff out Long's career. A version of Long in novel form is *All the King's Men*, by Robert Penn Warren. Both books are riveting.

FDR, Jean Edward Smith. Franklin Delano Roosevelt is the only president to have been elected four times, and that during the Great Depression and World War II. We can all learn from the strengths, weaknesses, personal skills and triumphs of FDR.

Truman, David McCullough. Truman was a small town, and some would say small time, haberdasher and county official. He was plucked from obscurity by the Kansas City, Missouri political machine to rise to the presidency, where he concluded World War II and faced up to the Korean War.

Boss: Richard J. Daley of Chicago, Mike Royko. The quintessential 20th Century urban political boss, Richard Daley made politics and government interchangeable, providing himself the power to decide elections, some would say even change the 1960 presidential election outcome.

ACKNOWLEDGEMENTS

Special thanks to Rick Brooks, co-founder of Little Free Libraries; Dick Simpson, author, professor, politician; and Mike Lawrence, retired director of the Paul Simon Public Policy Institute. These friends, deeply experienced in politics, government and civic life, commented extensively on the first draft. Invaluable. The following also made major improvements and corrections to this book. I am in the debt of all.

Robert Barry, retired Illinois and Midwest lobbyist

David Beal, retired business editor, St. Paul Pioneer-Press

Phil Gonet, retired lobbyist, deputy governor, utility CEO

Ray LaHood, former Member of Congress and U.S. Secretary of Transportation

Mary Kay Minaghan, lobbyist at City of Chicago and its City Council

Joan Parker, retired lobbyist and former Speaker of the Third House of Illinois

Anthony Sarros, former executive director of the Illinois Republican Party

Cal Skinner, former member of Illinois House of Representatives

Don Udstuen, former chief lobbyist, Illinois State Medical Society

Rep. Travis Weaver, Illinois House of Representatives

Dixie Zietlow, chief of staff to Illinois state Sen. Win Stoller

And a note of deep appreciation to Jessica Gray, my research associate, for invaluable support in myriad ways.

JIM NOWLAN
BIOGRAPHICAL SKETCH

Jim is a jack-of-all-trades in Illinois public affairs. He has been an Illinois legislator, statewide candidate, state agency director, senior aide to three Illinois governors, campaign manager for U.S. Senate and presidential candidates, professor, newspaper publisher and columnist.

Jim received his BA, MA and PhD degrees in political science, with minors in economics, from the University of Illinois at Urbana-Champaign. Whenever kicked out of government or politics, Jim has taken refuge as a senior fellow at the University's Institute of Government and Public Affairs. He has also taught in the American politics field at the U. of I. in both Urbana and Chicago, and Knox College.

Jim has been a "foreign expert" (visiting professor) with the School of International Relations and Public Affairs at Fudan University in Shanghai on three occasions. In China, Jim taught courses in American politics and public management. When in China, Jim gave invited lectures at major universities throughout China, including at Beijing, Nanjing, Suzhou and Northwestern (Xian) universities.

Jim is the author or co-author of eight books, including *Illinois Politics* (University of Illinois Press, 2010; under revision for a 3d edition, 2024) and *Fixing Illinois* (U. of I. Press, 2015). Jim recently completed a four-year term as member, then chair, of the Illinois Executive Ethics Commission.

Jim's 400 newspaper columns and other writings can be seen at jimnowlan.net.

ENDNOTES

1   Daniel Weltman, "Nasty, Brutish, and Short: Hobbes on Life in the State of Nature," 1000-Word Philosophy: An Introduction Anthology. Accessed February 20, 2023. https://1000wordphilosophy.com/2021/07/14/hobbes-on-the-state-of-nature/#_ftn2

2   Elizabeth Venstra, *1,001 Pearls of Life-Changing Wisdom: Insight on Identity, Truth, and Success.* (New York: Skyhorse Publishing, 2016).

3   Niccolò Machiavelli, *The Prince*, 1513.

4   Robert M. Sapolsky, *Behave: The Biology of Humans at our Best and Worst* (New York: Penguin Books, 2017).

5   David Easton, *The Political System*: *An Inquiry into the State of Political Science.* (New York: Knopf, 1964.)

6   "Lyndon B. Johnson: Master of the Senate." United States Senate, last modified 2023, https://www.senate.gov/about/origins-foundations/parties-leadership/johnson-b-lyndon.htm.

7   "Rutan v. Republican Party of Illinois." Oyez. Accessed February 20, 2023. https://www.oyez.org/cases/1989/88-1872.

8   For a more comprehensive discussion of this subject, see Dick Simpson and Betty O'Shaughnessy, *Winning Elections in the 21st Century* (Kansas: University Press, 2016).

9   "Did Money Win?" OpenSecrets, Following the Money in Politics, April 1, 2021. https://www.opensecrets.org/elections-overview/winning-vs-spending

10 James D. Nowlan, Samuel K. Gove, and Richard J. Winkel, Jr., *Illinois Politics: A Citizen's Guide*, (Urbana: University of Illinois Press, 2010), 29.

11 "Tribunes of the Plebs," UNRV Roman History, last updated 2023. https://www.unrv.com/government/tribunes-of-the-plebs.php

12 James David Barber, *The Lawmakers: Recruitment and Adaptation to Legislative Life* (Connecticut: Yale University Press, 1962).

13 Jesse Norman, *Edmund Burke: The First Conservative* (New York: Basic Books, 2013).

14 Doris Kearns Goodwin, Team of Rivals: The Political Genius of Abraham Lincoln (New York: Simon & Schuster, 2005).

15 Surface Coal Mining Land Conservation and Reclamation Act, 225 ILCS 720/1.01 to 720/9.08 (ILGA, June 1, 1980).

16 Ray LaHood and Frank Mackaman, *Seeking Bipartisanship: My Life in Politics* (New York: Cambria Press, 2015).

17 Terry Sanford, *Storm over the States*. (New York: McGraw-Hill, 1967).

18 NPR, *A Lobbyist by Any Other Name?* Podcast, 2:36, from an interview aired January 22, 2006, heard on *Weekend Edition Sunday*, https://www.npr.org/2006/01/22/5167187/a-lobbyist-by-any-other-name.

19 A Political Action Committee (PAC) is a private group that raises and distributes funds for use in election campaigns. Allowed to give a limited amount of money directly to a candidate, and spend unlimited amounts independent of coordination with a candidate campaign.

20 National Institute of Justice, "A Handful of Unlawful Behaviors, Led by Fraud and Bribery, Account for Nearly All Public Corruption Convictions Since 1985," June 5, 2020, https://nij.ojp.gov/topics/articles/handful-unlawful-behaviors-led-fraud-and-bribery-account-nearly-all-public

21 Robert Bolt, *A Man for all Seasons: A Play of Sir Thomas More*. (Oxford: Heinemann Educational Publishers, 1960).

22 "Electoral History of Abraham Lincoln." Wikipedia. https://en.wikipedia.org/wiki/Electoral_history_of_Abraham_Lincoln#cite_note-ILStateHouse-2 Last updated January 17, 2023.

23 Philo, L. Curtius, L. Hostilia Scaura, and P. Iunius Brutus. Restoring the Ancient Roman Virtues. 2019. Roman Republic: Res publica Romana, romanrepublic.org/roma/bibliotheca/roman-virtues/

24 Miller, Julie. "'A Republic if You Can Keep It': Elizabeth Willing Powel, Benjamin Franklin, and the James McHenry Journal." Unfolding History: Manuscripts at the Library of Congress (blog). 6 January 2022, https://blogs.loc.gov/manuscripts/2022/01/a-republic-if-you-can-keep-it-elizabeth-willing-powel-benjamin-franklin-and-the-james-mchenry-journal/

Printed in the USA
CPSIA information can be obtained
at www.ICGtesting.com
LVHW020030051023
760125LV00005B/645